W9-AUK-194

SPECIAL REPORTS

THE SYRIAN CONFLICT

BY MICHAEL CAPEK

CONTENT CONSULTANT
SAMER ABBOUD
ASSOCIATE PROFESSOR, HISTORICAL AND POLITICAL STUDIES
ARCADIA UNIVERSITY

An Imprint of Abdo Publishing | abdopublishing.com

abdopublishing.com

Published by Abdo Publishing, a division of ABDO, PO Box 398166, Minneapolis, Minnesota 55439.

Printed in the United States of America, North Mankato, Minnesota
082016
012017

Cover Photo: Ameer Alhalbi/AFP/Getty Images
Interior Photos: Burhan Ozbilici/AP Images, 4–5; Rodrigo Abd/AP Images, 7; Hussein Malla/AP Images, 9, 36–37; OPIS Zagreb/Shutterstock Images, 14–15; AP Images, 20, 22, 24–25, 39, 43, 67, 92; Shutterstock/Rex Features/AP Images, 27; Kirsty Wigglesworth/PA/AP Images, 29; Christophe Ena/AP Images, 35; Khalil Hamra/AP Images, 45; Manuel Balce Ceneta/AP Images, 49; Virginie Nguyen Huang/AP Images, 50–51; Dusan Vranic/AP Images, 56; Jack Guez/AFP/Getty Images, 59; Balkis Press/Sipa USA/AP Images, 60–61; US Navy, 69; Kyodo/AP Images, 71; Alexander Kots/Komsomolskaya Pravda/AP Images, 72–73, 86–87; Muhammed Muheisen/AP Images, 77, 81; Rachel La Corte/AP Images, 85; Vladimir Isachenkov/AP Images, 89; Lefteris Pitarakis/AP Images, 97; Natalia Sancha/AP Images, 99

Editor: Arnold Ringstad
Series Designer: Maggie Villaume

Publisher's Cataloging-in-Publication Data

Names: Capek, Michael, author.
Title: The Syrian conflict / by Michael Capek.
Description: Minneapolis, MN : Abdo Publishing, 2017. | Series: Special reports | Includes bibliographical references and index.
Identifiers: LCCN 2016945408 | ISBN 9781680783988 (lib. bdg.) | ISBN 9781680797510 (ebook)
Subjects: LCSH: Syria--Politics and government--21st century--Juvenile literature | Palestine--Politics and government--Juvenile literature. | Middle East--Politics and government--21st century--Juvenile literature.
Classification: DDC 956.05--dc23
LC record available at http://lccn.loc.gov/2016945408

CONTENTS

ARAB SPRING AND THE BOYS OF DERAA

The kids were young and full of curiosity, fun, and energy. The seven of them had been friends for as long as they could remember, growing up in the farming town of Deraa in southern Syria, not far from the border with Jordan. Similar to most teens, they spent a lot of time kicking around a ball after school, watching television, and sitting around talking and joking.

Many Syrian teenagers became vocal opponents to the regime in Syria as the Arab Spring movement spread across the region.

They had been seeing news reports on television about demonstrations in Egypt. The images were thrilling, with excited crowds singing, shouting, carrying signs, and demanding freedom from a cruel, repressive government.

In early 2011, a spirit of revolt was spreading through the Middle East. The uprisings were collectively known as the Arab Spring. The boys often wondered whether the fresh, invigorating spirit of rebellion would ever reach Syria. People in the region were tired of poor economic conditions, secret police, corrupt government officials, and unfair policies. The conditions had lasted for decades, and there was no change in sight. It was illegal to talk openly against the government of President Bashar al-Assad. Privately, the boys frequently expressed their and their families' anger and frustration. Already, in February,

ARAB SPRING

The term *Arab Spring* describes a movement that swept through many Arab nations between 2010 and 2012. The uprisings most often began as enthusiastic, loosely organized demonstrations in which people expressed their frustration and anger about poor economic conditions or repressive government policies. In some places, the movement led to the removal of ineffective, corrupt governments and leaders from power, followed by efforts to replace them with more honest, effective ones. The movement began in December 2010 in Tunisia. It spread in the following months to Egypt, Libya, Yemen, and Bahrain.

a protest against Syria's police state had played out, mostly on social media. Called "A Day of Rage," the demonstration centered on the nation's capital, Damascus.[1]

While watching the news one day in February 2011, one of the boys suggested it might be fun to sneak out at night and secretly write the same kinds of Arab Spring slogans they saw on television on the walls of their school. Later, they met at the dark schoolyard. While lookouts kept watch, 15-year-old Bashir Abazed spray-painted the words, "It's your turn, Doctor."[2] To make perfectly clear that the message was meant to refer to the Syrian president, who had previously worked as a medical doctor, another

Graffiti soon became a major way for young Syrians to express their anger at the government.

boy wrote, "Down with Bashar al-Assad."[3] Laughing, the boys scattered, eager to see the reaction to their prank the following day.

Police came to the school the next morning, and they began questioning students at random. One of the students questioned was Nayaf, a 14-year-old friend of Bashir. During harsh questioning, he broke down and gave the police the names of the other boys, including Bashir.

Local authorities then turned the boys over to the Palestinian Security Branch, a particularly brutal and feared arm of Syria's state security force. Blindfolded and terrified, Bashir and the other boys were taken to a prison in Damascus, where they suffered weeks of physical and psychological torture.

THE FLAMES OF OPPOSITION

During the ordeal, the boys' families were given no information. For weeks, they did not even know where their sons were. The families staged a protest march, demanding information and humane treatment from local government officials. When hundreds of people marched to confront the local governor, armed security forces met

By March 2011, protests had spread throughout the city of Deraa.

them in the street. Protesters began shouting anti-Assad slogans, and security officers fired into the crowd, killing two people.

Authorities finally released Bashir and the others. The boys were weak, exhausted, and battered after weeks of torture and beatings. By that time, the story of the boys of Deraa had captured the attention of the entire country. Nonviolent antigovernment demonstrations were exploding throughout Syria, and security forces kept busy trying to stop them.

"IN EGYPT AND TUNISIA THEY CAN DEMONSTRATE SHOWING THEIR FACES, TAKE PHOTOS, AND PUT THEM ON FACEBOOK. WE CAN'T DO THAT. WHEN WE ASK SOMEONE TO COME TO THE STREETS, THEY SAY, 'YOU ARE ASKING US TO COMMIT SUICIDE.'"[4]

—A SYRIAN DEMONSTRATOR

A few weeks later, 13-year-old Hamza al-Khateeb was marching in the streets of Deraa, demonstrating with his family. Government agents began shooting into the crowd. During the chaos, Hamza was separated from family members and disappeared. No one saw him again until a month later, when he was returned to his family dead. His neck had been broken and his body showed signs of torture. Deraa exploded into protests, and in the weeks that followed, the city, besieged by government soldiers and tanks, became the focal point of military action. As Middle East expert John McHugo wrote, "A point of no return was passed, after which Syria became predestined to descend into chaos and civil war."[5]

The transition away from nonviolent demonstrations toward an armed struggle happened in stages. Journalist Reese Erlich reported that by July, members of Syria's security organizations and even some soldiers in the Syrian army became disturbed and disillusioned that officers were ordering them to shoot into crowds of unarmed citizens. Many men began deserting and joining groups of other defectors. These highly trained and well-armed fighters formed the Free Syrian Army (FSA), which later would become the backbone of the rebellion. Early on, though, they acted as guards for demonstrators, shooting at

GETTING THE MESSAGE OUT

Demonstrators need to present their cause clearly and dramatically. Often simply scribbling slogans on signs or in public places works. Even a single word seen by enough people can inspire unity and raise awareness. In 2011, protesters in Damascus wrote the word *freedom* on 5,000 ping-pong balls and dumped them out in a busy city park.[6] Government security officers spent hours trying to round them up.

and skirmishing with government forces that attacked otherwise peaceful demonstrators. Some protesters began arming themselves in self-defense, and occasionally they threw rocks. These developments heightened government retaliation and made it easier for the government to claim extremists were leading the rebellion.

The intensity level and frequency of engagements increased quickly after that. In October 2011, Assad government officials reported that 1,200 police, army, and other security personnel had been killed by protesters throughout Syria.[7] They also claimed extremists seized control of the demonstrations and began a purposeful campaign of violence against government security forces. In November, a group of FSA fighters attacked an air force base near Damascus. A month later, the group bombed a key Damascus security headquarters. Although thousands of protesters died in the following months throughout Syria as opposition

"THEY ARE NOT MY FORCES; THEY ARE MILITARY FORCES [THAT] BELONG TO THE GOVERNMENT. . . . I DON'T OWN THEM. I AM PRESIDENT. I DON'T OWN THE COUNTRY, SO THEY ARE NOT MY FORCES."[8]

—BASHAR AL-ASSAD, WHEN ASKED IN A DECEMBER 2011 INTERVIEW WHAT HE THOUGHT ABOUT THE USE OF FORCE AGAINST SYRIAN CITIZENS

against the Assad regime spread and government violence escalated, the government released no statistics about how many civilians were killed.

By 2016, the war in Syria had morphed into a conflict far more monstrous and complex than the boys in Deraa could have ever imagined. From that local antigovernment demonstration, the situation grew into a vicious civil war. Eventually it became a struggle involving not only the people of Syria against the Assad regime, but also many other forces and groups, some from foreign countries, each with their own agendas and goals. The massive humanitarian crisis caused by the war came to affect countries in the region and around the world.

THE HIGH COST OF CONFLICT

By March 2016, an estimated 470,000 people had died, and nearly 2 million had been wounded as a result of the Syrian conflict. Almost 5 million refugees had left Syria and 11 million more had been displaced, forced from their homes to seek refuge wherever they could inside Syria. Humanitarian agencies estimated 70,000 Syrians had already died from a lack of shelter, medical services, food, water, and sanitation.[9]

CHAPTER TWO

THE DEEP ROOTS OF TURMOIL

The violence happening in Syria and the Middle East is nothing new. The land called Syria today has been the scene of warfare, conquest, and rebellion since ancient times. For centuries, its geographic position at the eastern end of the Mediterranean Sea has attracted traders and travelers looking for a good place to set up shop. It has also drawn those on their way to other places farther east in Persia, India, and China. Syria was always a destination and a gateway, a place where great empires met for battle.

The armies of the Aramaeans, Assyrians, and Babylonians clashed in Syria. All of them ruled for a time, before falling to Alexander the Great, whose

The ruins of temples and other ancient buildings can still be seen in many parts of Syria.

armies brought Greek rule to the region in 332 BCE. The Greeks brought some degree of order, building roads and cities, before falling themselves to the mighty Roman Empire. The Romans ruled from approximately 64 BCE until 636 CE, when a different kind of army swept through the region. Muslim warriors spread their new religion of Islam across the Middle East and Europe. The capital of the empire they forged was moved from Damascus in Syria to Constantinople—today known as Istanbul, Turkey. In the final phase of this rule, known as the Ottoman Empire, Islamic caliphs ruled Syria for more than 400 years. The empire finally collapsed and shattered into many smaller nations in the 1900s after the two world wars.

QUEST FOR INDEPENDENCE

In 1916, while World War I (1914–1918) raged in Europe, Arab nations were hungry for self-rule after years of harsh Ottoman control. Syrians and other Arabs joined forces with the two great military powers in the Middle East at the time, the United Kingdom and France, against the faltering Ottoman Empire. In return, it was assumed that

MORE TO THE STORY

THE CRUSADES: INVASIONS FROM THE WEST

The Crusades were a series of European military invasions of the Middle East during the Middle Ages. They were inspired by Christian fervor to recapture the so-called Holy Land from Muslims who had conquered these regions during the Arab conquests. Crusaders arrived in Syria in approximately 1096 CE and fought with Muslims on and off for the next 400 years to take control of Jerusalem, Damascus, and other places important in the Christian faith. Between the violent clashes, the Crusades served to open the door between East and West for trade and the exchange of ideas and cultures. Some historians believe the wars also inspired feelings of hatred, aggression, and distrust between Muslims and Christians that still exist today. Others believe popular culture and mass media have continued to perpetuate such ideas and the Crusades themselves have little or no effect on Muslim–Christian relations today.

after the war, Syria and other Arab countries would obtain their freedom from foreign domination.

Following their victory in the conflict, France and the United Kingdom drew a new map that divided Greater Syria into separate states under their control. France took Syria and Lebanon, and the United Kingdom claimed Jordan and Iraq. Palestine was to be governed by an international regime. The Sykes-Picot Agreement, as the deal was called, created a new Middle East by ignoring promises made to Arab and tribal leaders and instead gave full control to the French and British. The result was a smoldering cauldron of discontent among various ethnic and religious groups, who felt marginalized and separated by what they considered artificial borders. As John McHugo explains, "To this day," the betrayal is still

THE PALESTINIAN QUESTION

In 1917, the United Kingdom sponsored the establishment of a Jewish nation in Palestine. Arabs already living in Palestine violently opposed the plan, and other Arab nations, including Syria, united behind them. Until 1948, fighting continued over land both sides considered theirs by divine right. In that year, Israel, backed by the United States and other Western nations, prevailed. It became a new Jewish nation in Palestine and sent 700,000 Palestinians into exile.[1] Clashes continued, including the Arab-Israeli War of 1967, in which Israel took the strategic Golan Heights from Syria. The issue still fuels resentment in Syria and the Middle East today.

"remembered with bitterness in Syria and other Arab countries."[2]

During World War II (1939–1945), the French once again promised Syrians independence in exchange for their help. When the French still refused to relinquish their control after the war, Syrians stormed the capital in Damascus. The mass demonstrations grew violent, and French forces bombed the city, killing more than 400 people.[4] Such attacks only strengthened Syrians' determination to be free of foreign overseers. Finally, in 1946, France withdrew all troops and turned Damascus

ECHOES OF THE PAST

Some people see bitter echoes of the past in the Arab Spring demonstrations. When the French marched into Damascus in the summer of 1920, they broke resistance by violently attacking people who did not want another military government. Demonstrations continued and erupted in 1925 in another violent rebellion. Much like the 2011 protests, the uprising was violently attacked by a repressive government with a powerful military.

"WHAT HAPPENED IN THE IMMEDIATE AFTERMATH OF [WORLD WAR I] CREATED A LEGACY OF MISTRUST OF THE WEST WHICH SUBSEQUENT HISTORY WOULD REPEATEDLY COMPOUND. TODAY'S INABILITY OF THE WEST TO PREVENT SYRIA FROM DESCENDING INTO THE DARKNESS OF CIVIL WAR—AND ITS FAILURE TO FIND A WAY TO BRING THE CIVIL WAR TO AN END—WILL ONLY HAVE INCREASED THAT MISTRUST YET FURTHER."[3]

—JOHN MCHUGO

over to the Syrians. Syria was a free and independent nation for the first time.

The Syria that emerged from the grip of Ottoman rule was a mere shadow of its former self. It was now only approximately the size of North Dakota. The land once know as Greater Syria, or the Levant, was vast, spreading all the way from the Mediterranean Sea into modern-day Lebanon, Israel, Palestine, Jordan, and Iraq, as well as the Antakya region of Turkey and the Sinai Peninsula of Egypt. What was still left after 1946 was divided into several independent nations: Syria, Lebanon, Jordan, Iraq, and Turkey.

The new Syrian nation was fragile, or as historian Joshua Landis has called it, "a political orphan."[5] It had no powerful allies and was overshadowed by large and antagonistic neighbors. Turkey in the north, Iraq in the east, and Jordan in the south were strong militarily and politically, and each had reasons to hope Syria might fail. Zionist militias in Palestine, on Syria's southern border, created civil unrest against Syria's Arabs.

British troops, allied with France, captured the ancient Syrian city of Palmyra during World War II.

Between 1946 and 1970, Syria struggled internally. Control of the government changed hands 20 times, with 11 presidents and four distinct constitutions. Military coups became commonplace. Desperate for stability, Syria merged with Egypt to form the United Arab Republic in 1958. But it backed out of the partnership in 1961 when it became clear powerful Egyptian political leaders intended to run everything. In 1963, plans for another merger, this one between Syria and Iraq, failed to gain enough support in either nation. Syria's political uncertainty continued.

WHO ARE THE ARABS?

In earlier centuries, only people who lived on the Arabian Peninsula were called Arabs. Today, however, the term is typically used to refer to any people who speak the Arabic language. It is also often generally assumed that the term refers to people living in the 22 countries belonging to the Arab League. Together, these nations had a combined population of slightly more than 385 million in 2014.[6] Broadly speaking, Arabs are all people living in the Middle East, except for Persians, Kurds, Israelis, and Turks. Religion has little to do with why a person is called an Arab, even though most Arabs—approximately 93 percent—are Muslims.[7] Some practice other religious faiths, including Christianity and Judaism.

Egyptian president Gamal Abdel Nasser was elected in 1958 as the first leader of the United Arab Republic.

CHAPTER THREE

THE ASSADS— THE LIONS IN DAMASCUS

After decades of confusion, in 1970 a strong leader finally emerged. Former fighter pilot Hafez al-Assad was an air force general and the country's defense minister. He ordered armed troops into government offices all over Damascus, including that of president Salah Jadid. The reins of power were once again passed. This time, a new regime took control without firing a single shot.

Hafez al-Assad had been among a group of army officers who seized power of the Syrian government in 1963, and over the years he continued to play a

The rise of Hafez al-Assad marked the beginning of his family's decades-long control over Syria.

leading role in establishing the Baath Party as Syria's leading political force. When he took over sole control of the country in 1970, Syria was in a state of economic and political chaos. The Six-Day War (1967) left Israel occupying the Golan Heights and a strategic high point on Mount Hermon that overlooked Damascus. Missiles and other weapons abandoned there by the Syrians could at any time be used to obliterate the capital city.

THE BAATH PARTY

Two Syrian teachers, a Christian and a Sunni Muslim, founded the Baath political party in the 1930s. The goal of their philosophy was the creation of a new system that ignored religious and social divisions, instead championing Arab pride and unity. The Baath Party became Syria's leading political party in the 1950s. It was the party adopted by Hafez al-Assad. Baathists have held power in Syria ever since.

Assad, whose name means "lion" in Arabic, used the ongoing conflict with Israel to make a wartime emergency law permanent. The law allowed Hafez to clamp down on every element of society and government as he took steps to prevent a future coup against his regime. He made himself commander in chief of the military and installed a network of police and security agencies answerable only to him. He placed family members and close supporters

Hafez, *seated at right*, sat with his wife and children for a portrait in 1992. Bashar, *standing, second from left*, would eventually succeed his father.

in positions of power, particularly in the military and state security.

During Hafez al-Assad's years in power, Syria improved in many ways. The regime brought literacy, education, electricity, and modern water and sanitation services to millions of people who had never had them before. It built dams, roads, railroads, hospitals, schools, and universities. Women could have independent careers, including positions in the government and military.

At the same time, the Assad regime became one of the most repressive and corrupt in the region. Dragged down by favoritism, bribery, and the exploitation of the poorer classes by a small, rich upper class, the Syrian economy

SHREWD MOVES

Although Hafez al-Assad was an Alawite Muslim, he allowed Sunni Muslims to operate the most profitable business ventures in the nation, making them wealthy and transforming many of his former enemies into allies. He even added Sunnis to his cabinet, including key posts such as foreign minister, defense minister, and vice president. Such moves strengthened his family's hold on power and deflected criticism that the regime was sectarian.

never flourished. The regime also suppressed basic freedoms and systematically used secret police and violence to control people and suppress any sign of opposition.

Among the most brutal Hafez crackdowns was carried out against a group called the Muslim Brotherhood in the 1980s. In 1979, extremists from the group attacked a Syrian military school, killing 83 cadets. After an assassination attempt against Assad sponsored by the Muslim Brotherhood failed, the president ordered the killing of more than 800 political prisoners.[1] In February 1982, Hafez ordered 12,000 troops and heavy weapons to Hama, Syria's fourth-largest city and the center of Muslim Brotherhood resistance. The attack lasted 27 days. The army flattened the city, killing between 10,000 and 25,000 people, the majority of whom were innocent civilians.[2]

FROM DAMASCUS SPRING TO ARAB SPRING

Bashar al-Assad was not supposed to follow his father as leader of Syria. The intended heir was to have been Hafez's older son, Basil. Handsome and athletic, Basil was his father's favorite, but he died in a car crash in 1994. Almost immediately, Hafez began preparing Bashar to take the reins of power, a process that continued for the next six years. When Hafez died suddenly of a heart attack in 2000, Bashar was ready to assume the role of president of Syria.

Bashar and his wife, Asma, met with many Arab and Western leaders in his first years in office, including Queen Elizabeth II of the United Kingdom.

Bashar had been an eye doctor, educated in London, England, and working in the Syrian military. He reportedly had no interest in politics. Shy as a child, the soft-spoken Bashar seemed to most observers much too refined and mild-mannered to fill his ferocious father's shoes. At age 34, Bashar was also too young, according to the Syrian constitution, to be president. The Syrian parliament solved that problem by simply changing the constitution.

Bashar's first months in power were extraordinary. He encouraged an open public discussion about reforms people would like to see, and in his first speech to the nation, he spoke about democracy, free speech, free press, government accountability, and the need for constructive criticism. Such words had rarely been heard from a leader in Syria. Bashar introduced the nation to Internet access and satellite television. As a special show of good will, Bashar ordered the release of 600 political prisoners locked up by his father.[3] Hopes soared and people started referring to the refreshing new openness as the Damascus Spring.

Then, just as suddenly as it had appeared, the progress halted. One year after taking office, Bashar suddenly ordered the arrest and imprisonment of ten of the country's most vocal political activists. The secret police began shutting down public discussion groups and forums. The result, as Sarah Leah Whitson, Middle East director at Human Rights Watch described it, was a return to the days of Hafez:

> *Whether Assad wanted to be a reformer but was hampered by an entrenched old guard or has been just another Arab ruler unwilling to listen to criticism, the outcome for Syria's people is the same. . . . Assad's record after 10 years is that he has done virtually nothing to improve his country's human rights record.*[4]

SYRIAN ACCOUNTABILITY

In 2003, the United States enacted the Syria Accountability and Lebanese Sovereignty Restoration Act, a set of sanctions and restrictions imposed by the United States against Syria and the Bashar al-Assad regime. The sanctions essentially halted diplomatic relations between the United States and Syria, as well as the export of products from the United States, except food and medicine, to Syria. The act also prohibited US businesses from investing or operating in Syria. Imposing sanctions was a way of backing up accusations by the George W. Bush administration in 2002 that Syria was guilty of sponsoring terrorism and committing inhumane practices.

Yet Bashar's hold on power only strengthened in the early 2000s, even as Human Rights Watch in 2010 still ranked Syria at or near the bottom in multiple categories, including press freedom, democratic government, and economic performance. Bashar continued to win reelection, mainly because, according to the constitution, he was the only person allowed to run. In 2009 and 2010, the United States and other Western nations attempted to improve relations with Syria that had eroded. The US Embassy in Damascus spoke of attempting a "reengagement," and diplomats reported "positive first steps," hints they saw that Bashar was about to change his ways and become more democratic.[5]

FAMILY MATTERS

As Hafez did before him, Bashar surrounded himself with family members from his earliest days in power. Aside from his brother Maher, who was commander of the Republican Guard military group, Bashar made his brother-in-law Assef Shawqat his deputy chief of staff. Shawqat was killed in 2012. Bashar's cousin Rami Makhlouf is a business tycoon who owns Syria's largest cell phone company. He has used the company to monitor the phone and web activities of millions of Syrians. Makhlouf's brother, Hafez, was a security chief in Damascus until 2014 when he was dismissed and left the country for Belarus.

At the same time, however, the Syrian economy was in shambles. Unemployment and poverty were extremely high. These poor economic circumstances played an important role in setting the stage for a civil uprising.

Under the Assads, Syria's economy suffered greatly. Smuggling became the norm. Products such as butter, tea, sugar, and bananas had to be smuggled into Syria from Lebanon and Jordan. The corruption deepened as time went on, creating a rich upper class of people who took advantage of the situation. The Assad family encouraged the corruption, as it helped keep them and their wealthy supporters in power. The corrupt system, which denied a large percentage of Syria's people opportunities to improve their lives, caused deep anger and hostility. As Middle East analyst Anna Borshchevskaya explained in 2010, "A decade into Bashar al-Assad's rule, the Syrian economy is languishing. The police state Bashar inherited from his father, Hafez, continues to obstruct any kind of reform whether in the political or economic spheres."[6]

Still, in January 2011, as Arab Spring demonstrations were bringing down corrupt leaders in Tunisia and Egypt, Bashar remained confident. He assured an interviewer that

"OUR ENEMIES WORK EVERY DAY IN AN ORGANIZED, SYSTEMATIC AND SCIENTIFIC MANNER IN ORDER TO UNDERMINE SYRIA'S STABILITY. WE ACKNOWLEDGE THAT THEY HAVE BEEN SMART IN CHOOSING VERY SOPHISTICATED TOOLS IN WHAT THEY HAVE DONE; BUT AT THE SAME TIME WE REALIZE THAT THEY HAVE BEEN STUPID IN CHOOSING THE COUNTRY AND THE PEOPLE, FOR SUCH CONSPIRACIES DO NOT WORK WITH OUR COUNTRY OR OUR PEOPLE."[7]

—BASHAR AL-ASSAD IN A SPEECH BEFORE THE SYRIAN PARLIAMENT, MARCH 30, 2011

"PRESIDENT ASSAD IN OUR JUDGMENT . . . HAS LOST THE ABILITY, THE CREDIBILITY TO BE ABLE TO UNITE THE COUNTRY AND TO PROVIDE THE MORAL CREDIBILITY TO BE ABLE TO GOVERN IT. PURELY AS A MATTER OF REALITY, IF THE WAR IS TO END IT IS IMPERATIVE THAT THE SYRIAN PEOPLE AGREE TO AN ALTERNATIVE IN TERMS OF THEIR GOVERNANCE."[9]

—US SECRETARY OF STATE JOHN KERRY

no such protests or rebellions could occur in Syria. His people had no desire or reason to rebel. "Syria is stable," he said. "This is the core issue . . . at the end we are not Tunisians and we are not Egyptians."[8]

Six weeks later, protests in Deraa set off antigovernment demonstrations throughout Syria. And, like his father had done, Assad gave orders to violently crush the dissenters rather than trying to peacefully resolve their grievances.

Protestors chanted against the Tunisian regime in January 2011, sparking a movement that soon spread to Syria.

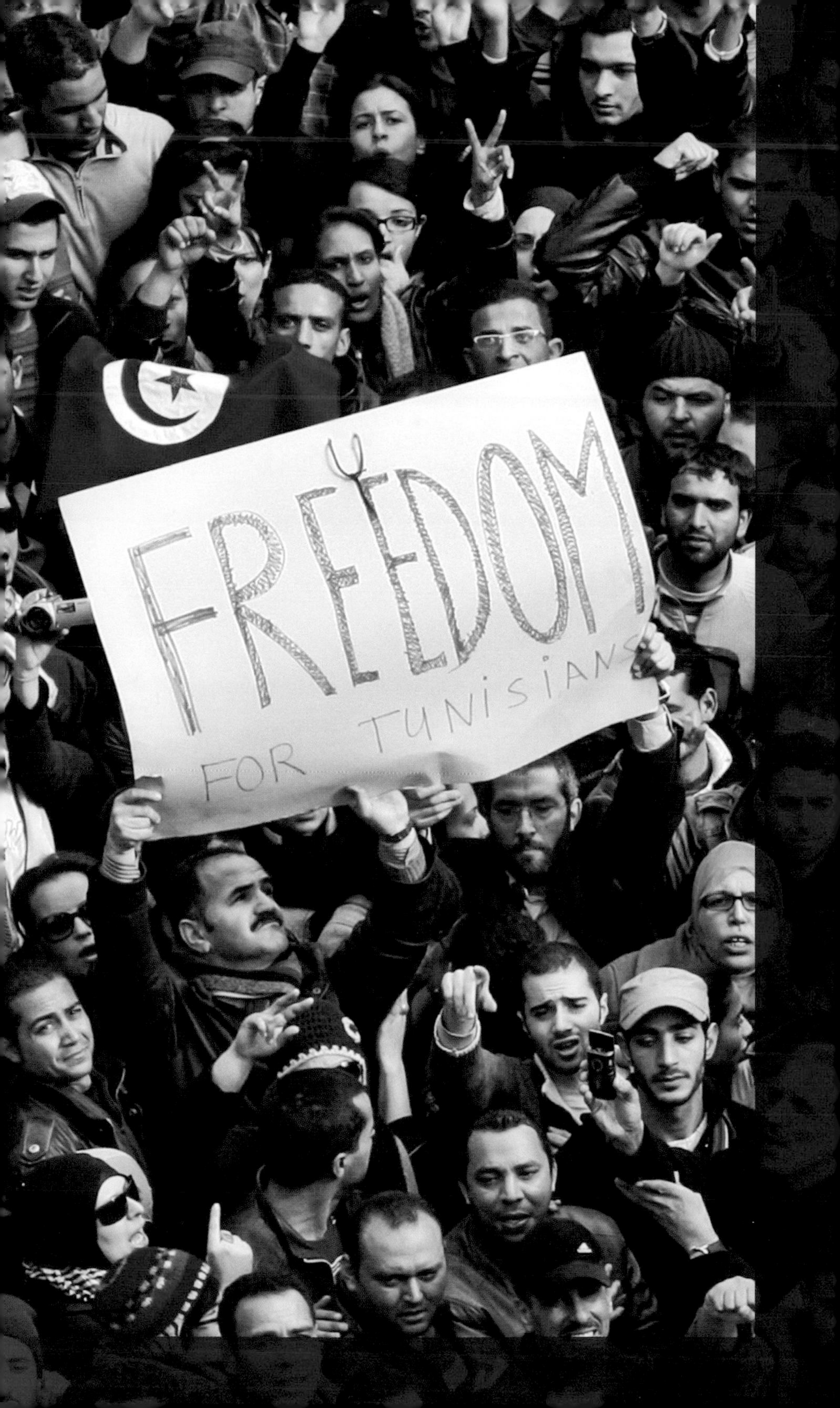
FREEDOM
FOR TUNISIANS

CHAPTER FOUR

A CONSTANTLY SHIFTING WAR

Syrian military and security forces continued violent attacks against protesters and organized opposition groups through 2011 and into 2012. The government's response intensified, reacting to what Bashar al-Assad called "terrorism" and "armed criminal gangs."[1] The death toll rose to an estimated 60,000 by the end of 2012.[2] By the summer of 2013, the number of dead reached 113,735. Of that number, 11,420 were children age 17 and younger.[3]

In February 2011, the Syrian army focused attacks on a Sunni Muslim neighborhood in the city of Homs. Sunnis still remembered how Hafez had leveled the city of Hama in 1982. So, when the armed resistance to the government began in 2011, large numbers of Sunnis

Syrian troops patrolled a burned-out building in Deraa in March 2011.

organized to fight Syrian security forces. Homs soon became a focal point of government attacks. Rockets and artillery shells began raining down on the city. Witnesses reported that many people who tried to escape the bombardment—even those who were not Sunnis or part of the opposition—were shot down by snipers. Others were captured and mistreated by Assad's troops.

Some of the Syrian army soldiers involved in the killing in Homs and elsewhere were disgusted by what they saw. People escaping battle areas reported seeing government officers shooting their own soldiers who refused to fire on innocent civilians. Many soldiers from the Syrian army began defecting and joining the opposition.

To stop news of vicious attacks getting out, the government banned foreign journalists from reporting on the fighting. The world witnessed the killing anyway,

BARREL BOMBS

Barrel bombs dropped by Syrian government forces during the first five years of the conflict killed thousands of Syrian civilians. Such bombs are technically simple. They are only large metal barrels packed with high explosives and sharp materials, such as nails. Pushed from the open doors of airplanes or helicopters, with little or no precise aiming, they explode on impact with tremendous force. Their use is considered by Human Rights Watch, the United Nations, and most other humanitarian organizations to be criminal and inhumane.

Syrian army defectors celebrated after joining protesters in January 2012.

thanks to modern technology. Hundreds of citizen journalists, self-appointed reporters with cell phones, took video footage, snapped photos, and posted descriptions on Facebook and YouTube. Horrific images from Homs and elsewhere stunned the world. The Syrian government could no longer deny it was killing its own people. Even so, President Assad called the online reports "fake information, voice, images, etc., they forged everything." He said he had given security forces direct orders "not to harm any Syrian citizens."[4]

Increased awareness brought a torrent of condemnation, and not only from the United States and other Western nations. Many Arab nations, too, called for Assad to stop his assault on his own citizens.

The Arab League, an organization of North African and Middle Eastern nations, suspended Syria's membership. Neighboring Turkey canceled more than $2.5 billion in trade and financial connections with Syria.[5] At the same time, when a resolution condemning the Assad government was brought before the United Nations (UN) Security Council in February 2012, Russia and China, two of Syria's few remaining allies, vetoed it.

WHO'S WITH THE OPPOSITION REBELS?

The opposition side of the conflict includes the FSA and conservative Muslim groups, including Ahrah al-Sham and the Nusra Front. Saudi Arabia, Turkey, and Qatar have trained and equipped the rebels. The Kurds, often with US air cover, continue to battle sectarian and government forces. The United Kingdom, France, and the United States back the opposition cause with some weapons, advisers, and air support, but the United States abandoned a $500 million effort to train rebels in October 2015.[6]

THE BATTLE WIDENS

By the summer of 2012, fighting had spread to parts of Aleppo and Damascus, Syria's largest cities. Scattered pockets of opposition troops began to come together. In July, the FSA, many of its members defectors from Assad's army, announced its intention to unify scattered groups and militias that had been fighting separately. The FSA aligned itself with the Syrian

National Council (SNC). The group was organized in Qatar by influential Syrians in exile who hoped to gain international recognition and financial support for the opposition cause. The United States and more than 100 other countries responded, endorsing the SNC as the official representative body of the Syrian people.[7] Qatar, Saudi Arabia, Libya, Lebanon, Jordan, and Iraq sent weapons, and other supplies began arriving and were funneled to FSA soldiers via various routes, including Turkey.

After a few successes, the FSA began struggling. It was a loosely organized group of independently operating units from the beginning. But the main problem was its lack of firepower against the Syrian army's array of heavy weapons. Assad's troops were equipped with rockets, missiles, and large artillery pieces, many of them supplied by Russia.

WHO'S FIGHTING FOR THE ASSAD GOVERNMENT?

The Assad government side of the conflict includes the Syrian Army and various allied militia groups. Iran and the Iran-supported Lebanese Shia militia Hezbollah are fighting the rebels, and so are Shia militia fighters from Iraq and Afghanistan. Russia has supported Assad forces with money, advisers, and weapons. It has also lent direct support with aerial bombing between late 2015 and early 2016. China supports Assad but has not directly entered the war.

FROM THE HEADLINES

CHEMICAL WEAPONS IN SYRIA

Early in the morning of August 21, 2013, a strange bombardment began raining down on Ghouta, a neighborhood of Damascus. Witnesses described rockets that spread a green mist that choked people and sent them into horrific spasms before they died. Videos posted online showed hundreds of bodies of men, women, and children, killed by what experts later found to be a deadly nerve gas called sarin.

The United States and other countries blamed the Assad government, which quickly denied its forces had fired the rockets, even though the Syrian Army had a known stockpile of chemical weapons. Assad agreed to destroy all such weapons but at the same time blamed rebel forces that wanted to turn international opinion against his government. Another credible claim surfaced that al-Qaeda–backed terrorist groups were responsible. Investigators for the UN and other international groups, such as the Organization for the Prohibition of Chemical Weapons, conducted investigations during the next year and a half, but none were ever able to positively prove who was responsible for the Ghouta attack. The reports revealed several groups fighting in Syria could have done it. A UN report, too, found chemical weapons have been used many times since the conflict began

UN investigators looked into allegations of chemical weapons use in Syria.

"FRANKLIN ROOSEVELT ONCE SAID, 'OUR NATIONAL DETERMINATION TO KEEP FREE OF FOREIGN WARS AND FOREIGN ENTANGLEMENTS CANNOT PREVENT US FROM FEELING DEEP CONCERN WHEN IDEALS AND PRINCIPLES THAT WE HAVE CHERISHED ARE CHALLENGED.' OUR IDEALS AND PRINCIPLES, AS WELL AS OUR NATIONAL SECURITY, ARE AT STAKE IN SYRIA, ALONG WITH OUR LEADERSHIP OF A WORLD WHERE WE SEEK TO ENSURE THAT THE WORST WEAPONS WILL NEVER BE USED."[8]

—PRESIDENT BARACK OBAMA, SEPTEMBER 10, 2013

FSA leaders made urgent appeals for similar weapons, but the United States and other Western nations were reluctant to send more powerful, technically sophisticated weapons—such as Stinger antiaircraft missiles and rocket-propelled grenades—into the confused and unstable situation. Observers on the ground reported numerous factions and foreign groups, some of them unidentified, fighting inside Syria. The FSA's supporters did not want to risk having heavy weapons fall into the wrong hands. Eventually, for this reason, the United States stopped supplying rebels with anything other than food, medicine, and humanitarian aid. Despite their lack of weaponry, rebel forces managed to capture the town of Raqqa, in northern Syria. As they had from the beginning, Assad forces responded with an all-out bombardment of the city that killed and wounded many more innocent civilians than rebels.

Later, in 2014 and 2015, the United States and its allies began sending more powerful weapons to rebel forces. One weapon that had an immediate effect was the US-made BGM-71 TOW missile. These antitank missiles made it possible for FSA soldiers to destroy powerful Syrian Army tanks, which Russia supplied to the Assad regime. The program was coordinated and monitored by the US Central Intelligence Agency (CIA). CIA agents also trained and advised FSA fighters and helped ensure the

Antitank missiles allowed rebel forces to fight back against the regime's armored troops.

weapons were being used against Assad forces and not opposition fighters.

"IN THE PERIOD AFTER THE [ASSAD] REGIME FALLS, OUR MAIN GOAL IS TO CREATE AN ISLAMIC STATE THAT IS RULED BY THE KORAN. IT CAN HAVE CIVILIAN INSTITUTIONS, BUT NOT DEMOCRACY"[10]

—A LEADER OF ISLAMIC GROUP AL-NUSRA, APRIL 2013

The reason for such cautious oversight was already clear. Many of the fighters battling Assad's forces also belonged to diverse Sunni Muslim militia groups opposed to the West, such as al-Qaeda and al-Nusra. Some smaller groups, many of which were not Syrians, joined forces in 2013 to form the Jaysh al-Islam, or Islamic Front, which was being supplied by wealthy Saudi Arabia with weapons. This powerful coalition refused to join with the FSA because they believed the FSA was not guided by Sharia law, or strict Islamic principles. Al-Islam apparently saw little difference between the two warring sides. Things became especially worrisome when al-Islam posted a statement on social media declaring that its "jihadists will wash the filth of [Shia] from Greater Syria, they will wash it forever, if Allah wills it."[9] This reflected yet another twist in the increasingly complicated conflict. It appeared no longer to

MORE TO THE STORY

THE KURDS

The Syrian conflict is a fight for survival for many ethnic groups. The Kurds, for instance, are a large ethnic group, totaling approximately 25 to 30 million people, who live in Syria, Iraq, Iran, and Turkey.[11] They have suffered persecution and prejudice for many years in the Middle East as they have fought to carve their own place. Following World War I, when the victorious powers divided the region into new nations, the Kurds did not get a state of their own. Despite occasional uprisings between the 1960s and the 1980s, they were unable to unify and form an independent country.

Iraqi dictator Saddam Hussein became notorious for his harsh and violent efforts to control the Kurds living in Iraq. Finally, in 2003, the US invasion of Iraq created an opportunity for Kurds living there to establish their own largely self-governing region within northern Iraq, and they hope the same thing might happen in Syria. The Kurds have vigorously supported the opposition in its fight against the Assad regime and the Islamic State. By 2016, the Kurds still did not have their own country.

be only a civil war. It was taking on a religious component as well. This was supported by the fact that Shia-led Iran supported the Assad regime with fighters and weapons, whereas Sunni-dominated opposition to Assad had the strong support of Turkey, Saudi Arabia, Qatar, and Jordan.

Between 2014 and 2016, many Middle East analysts saw the Syrian conflict evolving into a proxy war. The word *proxy* refers to people or groups who are authorized or enlisted to act in place of another—in other words, to act as a substitute. In Syria, the United States supported its proxies, the FSA and assorted rebel groups, who best served US and allied interests. But many observers worried the US-supplied weapons were often used by rebels specifically against Russia-supplied tanks and aircraft. Russia's support of the Assad regime and its forces was no secret. So, the resulting conflict began to look more and more like a proxy war between Russia and the United States.

President Barack Obama insisted in October 2015, "We're not going to make Syria into a proxy war between the United States and Russia."[12] Jeff White of the Washington Institute for Near East Policy agreed. "It's a

President Obama spoke to reporters at the White House about the situation in Syria on October 2, 2015.

proxy war by happenstance," he said. "The rebels happen to have a lot of TOWs in their inventory. The regime happened to attack them with Russian support. I don't see it as a proxy war by decision."[13]

THE RELIGIOUS DIVIDE

To fully understand the Syrian conflict, it is necessary to understand the role religion has played and continues to play in it. Like other aspects of the crisis, religion is a complicated and frequently confusing element, even for the people who are directly involved. The situation in Syria did not begin as a sectarian conflict. But analysts now tend to agree the Syrian conflict has evolved into a fight based in part on religious issues.

At the core of much of the resistance to Assad's government, for example, is an issue of religion—the fact that President Assad and most of those in control of his government are Alawites. Syrian Alawites have been persecuted and discriminated against for centuries,

As the fighting in Syria intensified, it became clear that the struggle had an important religious dimension.

mainly because they do not strictly follow the guidelines of any particular mainstream religion. The basis of their faith is Shia Islam. They believe in the divinity of Ali, the Prophet Muhammad's cousin, which is where their name comes from. But centuries ago, Alawites also borrowed elements from Christianity and other religions and philosophies. The sect became less religious and more secular.

This marked Alawites as heretics or infidels in the eyes of devout Muslims and Christians. It put the sect on the fringes of societies that were based on strict adherence to traditional religious rules and rituals. To survive, Alawites formed tight-knit communities and practiced their religion in secret. But in time, suspicion about them formed, particularly among Sunni Muslims, which increased even more the sense of alienation felt by Alawites.

During the years of the French rule, the French encouraged Alawites to join the military. The Sunni majority did not embrace military service, but Alawites saw it as an opportunity to gain the prestige and political power they never had previously. Hafez al-Assad and the Baathists' rise to domination in Syria was a direct result of this.

MORE TO THE STORY

WHAT'S THE ISSUE? SUNNI VS. SHIA

Of the 1.5 billion Muslims in the world, approximately 90 percent are Sunni. Among Syrians, the figure is approximately 74 percent.[1] The name Sunni is taken from the phrase "Ahl al-Sunnah," or "People of the Tradition." This refers to the practices of the Prophet Muhammad, Islam's central figure. Shia make up the remainder of the world's Muslims. Shia, which is a shortened form of "Shiat Ali" or the "Party of Ali," claims Ali, Muhammad's cousin, was the rightful successor to the Prophet Muhammad following the prophet's death in 632 CE. Despite this difference of opinion, the two main divisions of Islam agree on the basics as set down in their holy book, the Koran. They also share a common statement of belief, or creed. It's called *shahadah*, roughly translated as, "There is no god but Allah, and Muhammad is the Messenger of Allah." The Shia, however, add an additional sentence: "Ali is the Friend of Allah. The Successor of the Messenger of Allah and his first Caliph."[2]

Syrian Sunnis were inspired in 1979 by the Shia Revolution in Iran. The revolution was a popular rebellion against the hated Shah Pahlavi, a secular leader whose government was replaced by one run by Shia Muslim clerics. Sunnis in Syria wanted to do something similar: incite a popular rebellion and replace an Alawite government with a pious Sunni Muslim one. The plan did not work. In 1982, Hafez crushed the Muslim Brotherhood uprising. But the deep sense of resentment many Sunnis still feel against Alawites and the Assad regime today is a direct result of it.

"THE GANGS OF SYRIA"

One Middle East scholar, Nicole Sedaca, has defined the Syria conflict as "a religious civil war."[3] Another, Gram Slattery, has described it as the "gangs of Syria," often battling one another as often as they fight the Assad regime.[4] The Sunni-Shia conflict has boiled to the surface and is driving much of what is happening in Syria. The difference between Sunnis and Shia seems slight to many non-Muslims, but to many Muslims the division is distinct and deadly serious.

The division explains, in part, the bewildering array of groups that observers describe alternately battling Assad, the rebels, and each other in many parts of Syria. It is well known that Shia-led Iran is helping fund Assad's brutal campaign against the rebel opposition. Two groups directly sponsored by Iran, Hezbollah and the Iranian Revolutionary Guards, have frequently staged attacks against Sunni fighters in Syria. At the same time, Sunni-led Saudi Arabia and Qatar are funding various Sunni opposition fighters. And al-Qaeda, another group organized to fight Shia Muslims and their supporters, has also been actively fighting against various elements of the Syrian Sunni opposition. Splinter groups and factions, whose names seem to change from day to day, come and go. They appear to merge, split, reassemble, collapse, and rise again. It is no wonder the conflict is so often described as chaotic and confusing.

"ISLAM IS A RELIGION OF PEACE, AS IS CHRISTIANITY, JUDAISM, AND ALL THE RELIGIONS I KNOW OF. SOME EXTREMISTS IN THE UNITED STATES HAVE MURDERED ABORTION DOCTORS OR BLOWN UP A FEDERAL BUILDING IN THE NAME OF CHRISTIANITY, BUT WE KNOW THEIR ACTIONS ARE ANTI-CHRISTIAN. AND SO IT IS WITH POLITICAL ISLAM."[5]

—AUTHOR AND JOURNALIST REESE ERLICH

Christians continued to live and attend church services in Damascus in 2013.

The religious divide also involves Christians. Only a few years ago, some two million Christians lived in Syria, making up approximately 10 percent of the population.[6] Christians have been in Syria since the days of Saint Paul in the first century CE. Because his ministry to spread Christianity began in Damascus, that city has always been sacred to Christians.

The Christian influence in Syria has remained strong ever since. Michael Aflaq, the founder of the Baath Party, was a Greek Orthodox Christian yet a champion of Arab nationalism. Antun Saadeh, another Christian, was founder of the Syrian Social Nationalist Party, which in 1934 pushed for the reuniting of Lebanon and Syria into one nation. However, since the Arab Spring uprising of 2011, many Christians have fled, fearing sectarian Islamic violence might soon target them.

In fact, hundreds of thousands of Christians have been displaced by fighting or left the country. Melkite Greek Catholic Patriarch Gregorios III Laham estimated more than 1,000 Christians were killed when entire villages were cleared and dozens of churches and Christian centers were damaged or destroyed during fighting by 2014.[7] Others fear it may be only the beginning. Christian and political leaders have even used the term *genocide* to describe the degree of violence aimed at Christians there by a group called the

"[ISIS FIGHTERS] ARE KILLING OUR PEOPLE IN THE NAME OF ALLAH AND TELLING PEOPLE THAT ANYONE WHO KILLS A CHRISTIAN WILL GO STRAIGHT TO HEAVEN: THAT IS THEIR MESSAGE. THEY HAVE BURNED CHURCHES; THEY HAVE BURNED VERY OLD BOOKS. THEY HAVE DAMAGED OUR CROSSES AND STATUES OF THE VIRGIN MARY. THEY ARE OCCUPYING OUR CHURCHES AND CONVERTING THEM INTO MOSQUES."[8]

—ARCHBISHOP ATHANASIUS TOMA DAWOD OF THE SYRIAC ORTHODOX CHURCH IN IRAQ, AUGUST 2014

Islamic State, also known as ISIS. In 2016, US secretary of state John Kerry stated:

> *We know that in areas under its control, [ISIS] has made a systematic effort to destroy the cultural heritage of ancient communities—destroying Armenian, Syrian Orthodox, and Roman Catholic churches; blowing up monasteries and the tombs of prophets; desecrating cemeteries.*[9]

The real issue at the heart of the Syria conflict, then, as recent events have revealed, was no longer only religious differences. It was the rise to power of radical groups, such as ISIS, who refused to accept the existence of any religion but their own and believed the annihilation of other faiths was their religious duty.

PERSECUTION OF THE DRUZE

The Druze, a secretive minority sect living in southern Syria, have been the subject of religious persecution by Islamic extremists. They are Shia, but their practices and methods are distinctly different from those of Sunnis and other Shia. Some Sunni groups have destroyed their shrines and places of worship and forced many to convert, whereas ISIS has attempted to wipe out the sect altogether.

Members of the Druze religious minority looked on as explosions rocked nearby villages in the midst of fighting in 2014.

CHAPTER SIX

THE RISE OF ISIS

In June 2014, ISIS released a video that showed a bulldozer pushing down a pile of sand that had formerly marked the border between Iraq and Syria. As the machine leveled the traditional crossing point, the camera moved to show a handwritten sign lying in the sand that read, "End of Sykes-Picot."[1] It referred to the secret agreement between France and the United Kingdom that created what many Arabs have long believed are illegal and artificial nations and borders in the Middle East. The video was ISIS's symbolic way of showing its intentions of wiping out old borders and starting over, creating its own borders in a new Middle East.

ISIS fighters often appeared in propaganda videos as they spread across Syria and Iraq.

ثم الإخوة: شريف، سعيد وأبو بصير

TECH-SAVVY TERRORISTS

Experts are constantly amazed at ISIS's skilled use of modern technology and mass media. The group makes the most of the Internet, frequently posting high-quality video of its grisly deeds. Its propaganda machine is particularly polished, too. ISIS produces a stream of images and stories on social media that present its message and brutal activities in a variety of ways. To its enemies, the message is one of terror and dread. To possible recruits, it seeks to make the group's actions seem exciting. Posts are translated into various languages to reach a maximum audience.

ISIS began in Iraq. It was part of an opposition force aligned with al-Qaeda, united against US occupation after the US invasion of Iraq in 2003. It was headed by rebel leader Abu Bakr al-Baghdadi, noted during the war for his use of excessive brutality aimed at anyone who opposed him, sometimes even including other Islamic fighters. Al-Qaeda in Iraq was largely destroyed by US forces in 2007 and 2008, but it reemerged under al-Baghdadi as the Islamic State of Iraq in 2011 when the US military withdrew from Iraq. As soon as the Syrian uprising began, ISIS jihadists easily moved across the border and began fighting Assad's Syrian army and other groups for control.

The al-Baghdadi–led group had some early successes in Syria, capturing several towns and killing and terrorizing their citizens. ISIS received financial backing from Saudis

MORE TO THE STORY

WHAT'S IN A NAME?

Most people assume that ISIS stands for Islamic State in Syria. It can, but to the members of the terrorist group itself the last letter actually stands for *Sham*. That's an Arabic word that means "on the left." In Muslim tradition, places were described in terms of their direction from Mecca, the city at the center of the Islamic universe. Facing west from Mecca, the vast land on one's left was Greater Syria—the land ISIS is fighting to reunify into a vast Islamic state. Some people, including President Obama, prefer to use the acronym ISIL, which stands for Islamic State in the Levant. The term *Levant*, which means "rising," is a French term describing Greater Syria.

Another name that has become popular among ISIS's enemies is *Daesh*. It's an acronym for the Arabic words for Islamic State of Iraq and Sham. ISIS supposedly hates being called *Daesh* because it sounds like an Arabic word that means "to stomp on" or "trample," which is exactly what many people in the Middle East believe the Islamic State is trying to do to them.[2]

and other wealthy supporters in the region, but it also raised funds from protection money its fighters extorted from businesses in the areas they overran. Kidnapping became an important source of money, too. The group would hold captives until families paid ransoms for their release. It frequently staged brutal and bloody executions of captives whose relatives would not or could not pay. Such brutal tactics became ISIS's trademark.

In 2013, al-Baghdadi officially announced a change in his organization's name to the Islamic State of Iraq and al-Sham, to better fit the group's aims of establishing an Islamic state that ignored former national borders. Its soldiers, many of whom gained experience fighting US troops in Iraq, were tough and unrelenting. They wanted to establish Islamic control over the places they captured.

When ISIS took the town of Raqqa, it imposed strict Sharia law. Citizens were forced to attend prayers five times each day in the town's mosque. Women were forced to wear a niqab, a full-face veil, in public. Smoking and drinking alcohol were prohibited. Anyone found breaking the laws was beaten or killed. ISIS also took control of local services and resources, including water. In Syria's arid climate, this gave them tremendous power not only over local citizens, but also over other fighting groups.

"O MUSLIMS EVERYWHERE . . . YOU HAVE A STATE AND *KHILAFAH*, WHICH WILL RETURN YOUR DIGNITY, MIGHT, RIGHTS, AND LEADERSHIP. IT IS A STATE WHERE THE ARAB AND NON-ARAB, THE WHITE MAN AND BLACK MAN, THE EASTERNER AND WESTERNER ARE ALL BROTHERS. . . . SYRIA IS NOT FOR THE SYRIANS, AND IRAQ IS NOT FOR THE IRAQIS. THE EARTH IS ALLAH'S."[3]

—ABU BAKR AL-BAGHDADI, LEADER OF THE ISLAMIC STATE

THE NEW FACE OF TERROR

In February 2014, ISIS and al-Qaeda officially split, marking the end of years of disputes between the leadership of the two groups. The main issue had to do with control of Jabhat al-Nusra, an al-Qaeda group fighting in Syria. ISIS and al-Nusra soldiers had frequently clashed while fighting in rebel-held regions of northern Syria. Observers noted al-Qaeda apparently had grown tired of ISIS's use of extreme methods, including beheadings, torture, and beatings, as well as bans on smoking and music.

The split did not significantly change the overall picture in Syria. By 2014, the conflict had become largely a stalemate between the Syrian government and the combined opposition forces. Each side took cities and land but was unable to gain the upper hand militarily. But the split with al-Qaeda may have empowered ISIS to take more decisive action in Iraq. It began a strong offensive against Iraqi forces in an effort to gain control of territory along the Iraq and Syria border. ISIS won a resounding victory in June 2014 when it took Mosul, one of Iraq's largest towns. Shortly after, al-Baghdadi's forces took the nearby city of Tikrit. "Not long ago," German magazine *Der Spiegel* reported, "ISIS was just one of many rebel groups fighting in the Syrian civil war. Now, it is spreading fear and violence across two countries, and its enigmatic leader Abu Bakr al-Baghdadi . . . and his fighters control an area in Syria and Iraq that is almost as big as Jordan."[4]

Days later, al-Baghdadi released a video in which he announced his formation of a new caliphate, or Islamic state, with himself as its Caliph Ibrahim. He also declared that henceforth ISIS would be known simply as the Islamic State. The proclamation shocked and enraged many Muslims worldwide. "The Islamic caliphate can't be restored by force," Sheikh Abbas Shuman, a leading Sunni Muslim authority said. "Occupying a country and

ISIS supporters marched in Mosul after the group seized the town in the summer of 2014.

killing half of its population . . . this is not an Islamic state, this is terrorism."[5] Al-Baghdadi did not deny the charge. In fact, he embraced it. "Terrorism is to worship Allah," he announced the next day. "Terrorism is to refuse humiliation, subjugation, and subordination. Terrorism is for the Muslim to live as a Muslim, honorably with might and freedom. Terrorism is to insist upon your rights and not give them up."[6]

Al-Baghdadi's announcement and the Islamic State's rise to power changed the whole complexion of the Syrian conflict. In August 2014, ISIS forces routed Kurdish fighters in northern Iraq and attacked villages where thousands of Syria's Yazidi, a non-Islamic religious minority, have lived for generations. Tens of thousands fled into nearby mountains, but thousands more who could not escape were reportedly massacred by ISIS. Hundreds more were later captured and enslaved by ISIS warriors, who cited Sharia laws that allow Muslim warriors to enslave nonbelieving captives.

ISIS'S GLOBAL REACH

Since declaring its caliphate in June 2014, ISIS has conducted or inspired at least 90 terrorist attacks in 21 countries other than Iraq and Syria. These attacks have killed at least 1,390 people and injured more than 2,000 others.[7] At least seven of the incidents happened in North America. One of the most deadly was in San Bernardino, California, in December 2015. A husband and wife team loyal to ISIS killed 14 and injured 21 others during an attack on a local health-care facility.[8]

On August 19, 2014, the group released a video showing the beheading of American journalist James Foley, who had disappeared in Syria more than a year earlier. Voices on the video also threatened to kill another captive journalist, Steven Sotloff. Two weeks later, the group executed Sotloff, too. Soon after, US planes began bombing specific ISIS targets in Syria and Iraq, the first such attacks since the war began. "This is the punch in the nose to the bully that we talked about on the playground," a US military official said of the attacks. "ISIS is the bully, and we just punched him in the nose."[9] President Obama promised Americans, "We will degrade, and ultimately destroy [ISIS] through a comprehensive and sustained counter-terrorism strategy."[10] ISIS spokesman Abu Muhammad responded by issuing a call for Muslims living in the West to mount attacks wherever they were. The call fit with ISIS's previous promise to move its brutal brand of terrorism beyond the borders of Syria and Iraq into the wider world.

Carrier-launched US aircraft, including F/A-18 Super Hornets, began striking ISIS targets in 2014.

FROM THE HEADLINES

ATTACKING HISTORY

Syria is home to approximately 6,500 ancient sites, ranging from Neolithic settlements to Roman ruins to medieval mosques and castles. A satellite survey done in 2015 of 1,450 of Syria's most important sites showed that one in four has been damaged during the conflict.[11] Some have been totally destroyed. The collateral damage caused by bombing, shooting, and shelling is to blame for much of it. But Syria's historic legacy is also under attack by purposeful destruction and looting by those who hate what the sites represent or who hope to make money by illegally selling Syria's treasures.

ISIS is among the worst offenders. It attacks sites with bulldozers and explosives and posts videos of the destruction. Reports of militants rampaging through museums and stealing ancient relics for sale have become commonplace, too. In 2015, ISIS captured Palmyra, one of Syria's most famous ancient cities. Soon, images appeared of the group blowing up the city's 1,900-year-old Temple of Baalshamin and the equally ancient Temple of Bel.

ISIS leaders claim the destruction and looting is religiously motivated. They believe it is their duty to destroy religious sites that honor or represent religions other then their own. ISIS also uses the sale of stolen art on the black market to help fund its military operations.

An arch in the ancient city of Palmyra before, *top*, and after, *bottom*, ISIS came to the area

CHAPTER SEVEN

A HUMANITARIAN CRISIS

In 2012, a 29-year-old man named Aamir and his family were trapped inside their house in Damascus by bombing. After days with nothing to eat or drink, he was forced to go out in search of food. In the street, members of the FSA stopped him and ordered him to join the opposition. When he refused, they told him, "The next time we see you, either you take your gun and stand beside us or you find someone to take your body."[1]

Seventeen-year-old Yusra Mardini and her older sister Sarah left Damascus in early August 2015, searching for safety from bombs and terror. In Turkey, the sisters boarded an inflatable raft meant for six that was loaded with 20 people. Only the sisters and

With large portions of their cities turned to rubble, the Syrian people faced extreme hardship as the war continued.

one other person aboard knew how to swim. Out on the wave-swept Mediterranean Sea, the boat began to sink. Yusra and Sarah jumped into the water and swam alongside. For hours, they pushed and tugged on the raft until it reached a small island off the coast of Greece.

A young husband and father, Faez al Sharaa, was stopped on a street in Deraa on his way to work in 2013 by a group of Syrian army soldiers. The soldiers accused Faez and three others of being terrorists. The terrified men stood at gunpoint, hands in the air, waiting to be shot. Suddenly, an old woman appeared and began pleading with the soldiers to let the men go. They were her son, her nephew, and her neighbor, she said. Faez had never seen the woman before. Incredibly, the soldiers turned and walked away. Faez will never forget the stranger who saved his life.

Aamir, Yusra, Sarah, Faez, and their families have one thing in common. They all managed to survive and escape the Syrian conflict and find refuge in the United States or another country. But not all of those seeking shelter have been able to find it.

The statistics are staggering. Since the conflict's beginning, more than 470,000 people have been killed and nearly 2 million more have been injured.[2] A total of 4.8 million Syrian refugees have been forced to leave the country, and 6.5 million are homeless or wandering inside Syria. And as of February 2016, the UN Office for the Coordination of Humanitarian Affairs (UNOCHA) has reported at least 13.5 million people in Syria are in urgent need of humanitarian assistance.[3]

CHILDREN USED IN COMBAT ROLES

The UN and Human Rights Watch have confirmed hundreds of children ages 14 to 17 were recruited by armed groups and served as fighters or in other combat roles during the Syrian conflict. Children were found to be with FSA units, the Kurdish YPG, ISIS, and the Nusra Front. Reports say children have served as snipers, spies, human shields, suicide bombers, and battlefield messengers. Another report said children in some places were offered free schooling, which in reality turned out to be military and weapons training.

The picture these statistics paint of life inside Syria is bleak. Life expectancy in Syria is estimated to have dropped by 20 years.[4] School attendance has gone down by more than 50 percent. Syria's economy has shrunk by an estimated 40 percent since 2011, leaving large numbers of Syrians with no jobs or regular income.[5] The result is what some observers are now calling "the worst humanitarian crisis of the twenty-first century so far."[6]

FROM THE HEADLINES

STARTING OVER

Like most refugees starting over in a new place, coming to the United States is not easy for Syrian refugees. In fact, when the Al Roustom family arrived in New Jersey in 2015, they had almost nothing but the clothes they were wearing. Parents Hussam and Suha and their two children moved into an apartment in Jersey City, New Jersey, furnished with donated furniture.

Back home, they had lived in Homs, one of Syria's most heavily bombed cities. The market where Hussam worked was destroyed, and so was the children's school. They had not been to school in four years. In Homs, the family was in constant danger of being shot by snipers or buried alive in collapsing buildings. That is why they fled with dozens of others on foot, crowded into a pickup truck, and rode across the Syrian Desert to reach Jordan. The trip from a refugee camp in Jordan to the United States was long and exhausting. The whole family is weary, but they are happy to be in a safe place. That does not remove the pain they feel in being separated from friends and relatives. The family does not even know whether some of them are still alive.

"I came here to live a life of dignity, and I feel lucky that we escaped. But I worry about the future of all Syrians," Hussam said. He worried that many Americans do not trust him. "I am not a terrorist," he says. "Syrians are not terrorists."[7]

Severely injured men, women, and children fled to refugee camps where conditions were little better than those in the horrific places they left behind.

World response to the crisis has been extraordinary. In response to the crisis, UN agencies appealed to donors in the United States in 2013 to give $6.5 billion—the biggest amount so far requested for a single humanitarian emergency.[8] Other nations around the globe have also sent or pledged billions in aid, including money, food, medical supplies, and many other things.

"THE MAJORITY OF THE SYRIAN PEOPLE—AND THE SYRIAN OPPOSITION WE WORK WITH—JUST WANT TO LIVE IN PEACE, WITH DIGNITY AND FREEDOM. AND THE DAY AFTER ANY MILITARY ACTION, WE WOULD REDOUBLE OUR EFFORTS TO ACHIEVE A POLITICAL SOLUTION THAT STRENGTHENS THOSE WHO REJECT THE FORCES OF TYRANNY AND EXTREMISM."[9]

—PRESIDENT BARACK OBAMA, REMARKS TO THE NATION, SEPTEMBER 10, 2013

Yet a great deal of help has not reached those who need it the most. Continued fighting in Syria has largely blocked the delivery of aid to civilians who remain under almost constant attack. That makes getting out of the way, not to mention getting out of the country, nearly impossible. Aid organizations report the war only adds to difficulties Syrians have faced for years, such as long-standing government repression and a system of bribes and price-fixing. Residents are forced to depend on tunnels and smugglers for daily goods and humanitarian aid. Groups such as the International Red Cross, Doctors Without Borders, the UN Children's Emergency Fund, and Human Rights Watch still work tirelessly to help suffering Syrians.

AID WORKERS ON THE FRONT LINES

Kayla Mueller, a young American aid volunteer, was captured by ISIS in 2013 and was reportedly killed in early 2015. Many others like her have been killed as well. UN aid agencies reported in 2016 that dozens of other workers have lost their lives in Syria. Mental and emotional distress is a serious problem, too. A 2015 poll of aid workers in war-torn areas found 79 percent of respondents stated they had experienced mental health issues, including post-traumatic stress disorder.[10]

THE REFUGEE DILEMMA

Since 2011, millions of Syrian refugees have managed to escape the violence in Syria. But getting out, in many cases, has presented a new set of problems. Leaving the country has meant dealing with border crossings. Many refugees have found themselves among millions of others looking for a place to go. Thieves, smugglers, and other criminals routinely prey on refugees, especially when they try to make plans for a risky boat crossing to free Mediterranean nations. Others escape only to be harassed by citizens or even arrested by security forces in other countries.

Nations bordering Syria—particularly Jordan, Lebanon, and Turkey—have become increasingly less welcoming, with stricter rules and shrinking refugee benefits. Some refugees who can afford a plane trip can go further afield, perhaps to Europe.

A majority of refugees have found sanctuary in the nations closest to Syria. By 2015, Turkey had taken in the most, approximately 2.7 million.[11] Approximately 14 percent of those lived in special camps, and the majority of them were children and teens. The small nation of Lebanon had accepted 1.1 million, 25 percent of its prewar population, and Jordan had taken in approximately 630,000 Syrians. Iraq had accepted 249,000, many of whom are former citizens who fled to Syria during the Iraq War (2003–2011).[12] In Europe, German officials said they would be willing to take 500,000 each year for the next several years.[13] The United Kingdom stated it planned to focus more on resettling vulnerable refugees who were already in camps in countries bordering Syria, rather than those who had already entered Europe.

The United States said in 2015 it would increase the number of Syrian refugees it would accept to 10,000 in

Refugee camps sprang up in Syria and neighboring countries to house those displaced by the violence.

the fiscal year beginning October 2015, from the fewer than 2,000 it had accepted in 2014. Some charities and aid organizations have criticized what they see as the United States' small commitment to the refugee crisis, compared with that of other nations. The Obama administration has pointed out that since the Syrian conflict began in 2011, the United States has donated more than $4.5 billion in humanitarian aid to Syria.[14] Most of it was spent on food, clothing, and medical supplies. Some money was also given to the governments of countries neighboring

Syria that are burdened with massive numbers of refugees. US officials say their policy of helping refugees stay close to their homes is better, in the long run, for refugees and their host nations.

"WHEN DID WE BECOME SO FEARFUL? THE SEPTEMBER 11 [2001] ATTACKS TAUGHT ME NOT TO LIVE IN FEAR OR GIVE IN TO TERRORISM. IF THE WORLD TURNS ITS BACK ON THE REFUGEES, THEY WILL BE FORCED TO RETURN TO SYRIA AND THEN THE ISLAMIC STATE WINS."[15]

—ALISON THOMPSON, A PARAMEDIC AND THE FOUNDER OF THIRD WAVE VOLUNTEERS, A GROUP WORKING WITH SYRIAN REFUGEES ON THE GREEK ISLAND OF LESBOS

But in places such as Jordan, the economy and social stability can become overwhelmed by millions of refugees. They have come not only from Syria but also from Palestine, Iraq, and various African nations and must compete for jobs and housing with citizens. The Jordanian government has expressed its disappointment regarding the lack of international assistance it has received.

The UN hosted a meeting in Geneva, Switzerland, in March 2016 to encourage nations to give and do more for Syrian refugee relief. In February, a similar conference in London raised $11 billion, and wealthy countries pledged to take in 178,000 of the 480,000 Syrians the UN wished to resettle.[16]

The refugee crisis also sparked debates about security. Host nations were concerned that terrorists, including those aligned with ISIS, could slip in alongside truly vulnerable refugees. Various nations, including the United States, have adopted methods of screening the people who apply for entry. But no method, no matter how strenuous, is foolproof. In November 2015, the governors of 30 US states agreed they would block the settlement of any Syrian refugees in their states.[17] They cited not only concerns about terrorists coming in, but also the threat of violence by US citizens against Muslims in general. As evidence, they pointed to incidents in which mosques were vandalized in some cities.

A solution to the Syrian refugee crisis will not be easy to find. Still, government, business, and civic leaders around the world must continue to work together to share information and resources. There are clearly many problems and dangers in helping refugees, but the worst option would be to do nothing. The real hope, and the ultimate solution to the humanitarian crisis, of course,

"IT IS TIME FOR THE WARRING PARTIES TO END THIS HORRENDOUS CONFLICT AND FOR THE WORLD POWERS WHO CAN INFLUENCE THE SITUATION TO ACT DECISIVELY. VIOLATIONS OF INTERNATIONAL HUMANITARIAN LAW ARE A CONSTANT AND TERRIBLE FEATURE OF THE WAR IN SYRIA. THESE VIOLATIONS LEAD TO UNIMAGINABLE AND UNNECESSARY SUFFERING."[18]

—INTERNATIONAL COMMITTEE OF THE RED CROSS PRESIDENT PETER MAURER, FEBRUARY 2016

would be an end to the violence that created the catastrophe in the first place.

In the United States, protests broke out in support of both sides of the refugee issue.

IMMIGRANT RIGHTS are a HUMAN RIGHT
LISTEN
VETS BEFORE REFUGEES
NO REFUG
HARLEY-DAVIDSON
MOTORCYCLES

WHAT'S NEXT?

In January and February 2014, the UN held a conference in Geneva to discuss the Syria conflict. But because not all sides involved in the war showed up, the meetings failed to accomplish much. The conflict went on.

Fighting in Syria in 2015 and early 2016 proved just how much had changed since 2011. The focus of the conflict seemed to have become less a struggle of the people of Syria against the Assad regime and more a concerted effort by everyone involved to contain ISIS. Throughout 2015, US and Syrian planes supported associated ground forces and stepped up attacks against ISIS. In September, at the request of President Assad, Russia joined the air assault against rebel units

By 2016, many of Syria's people were still trying to wait out the fighting in cities reduced largely to ruins.

and ISIS. The resulting tensions, when US planes bombed Assad forces and Russian planes bombed anti-Assad rebels, made some observers worry about worsening relations between Russia and the United States in the long run. Still, with Russia's help, the Syrian army managed to gain back a great deal of the territory it had lost to ISIS and rebel forces by January 2016. The Assad regime found itself in perhaps its strongest and most stable position in years. In March 2016, Russia halted its air support inside Syria, a move some analysts believed was a signal to Assad that it was time for him to begin looking for ways to end the war.

"NONE OF US ARE UNDER ANY ILLUSIONS. WE'RE ALL AWARE OF THE MANY POTENTIAL PITFALLS, AND THERE ARE PLENTY OF REASONS FOR SKEPTICISM. BUT HISTORY WOULD JUDGE US HARSHLY IF WE DID NOT DO OUR PART IN AT LEAST TRYING TO END THIS TERRIBLE CONFLICT WITH DIPLOMACY."[2]

—PRESIDENT BARACK OBAMA, COMMENTING ON A CEASE-FIRE AGREEMENT IN SYRIA THAT BEGAN ON FEBRUARY 22, 2016

In February, US secretary of state John Kerry announced the United States, Russia, and other nations had agreed to call a "cessation of hostilities" in Syria's civil war, to take effect the following week.[1] The cease-fire would also

With Russian air support, Syrian forces made significant gains against rebel troops in 2015 and 2016.

permit immediate access by humanitarian aid groups to areas inside Syria that had previously been too dangerous to enter.

On February 26, 2016, the UN Security Council unanimously adopted a resolution that ordered all parties to comply with the terms of the US-Russian deal. The cease-fire, which officially began on February 27, did not include attacks on certain terrorist organizations, particularly ISIS. Russian aircraft and Assad regime forces continued to attack after the cease-fire was in place, but they also attacked other opposition fighters, in direct violation of the cease-fire agreement. So did the FSA and other opposition groups.

"WE HAVE TWO OPTIONS: EITHER TO SURRENDER, OR TO DEFEND OURSELVES WITH THE MEANS AT OUR DISPOSAL. THE SECOND CHOICE IS THE BEST: WE WILL DEFEND OURSELVES."[3]

—SYRIAN FOREIGN MINISTER WALID MUALLEM

In practice, the truce was a partial cease-fire rather than a full stoppage of all violence. Yet from the start, all sides had expressed how difficult the challenge would be to sustain peace in a nation where hostilities had raged for five years. To the surprise of many people, despite occasional clashes, the truce held through April 2016.

As the partial cease-fire continued, representatives of various groups engaged in the conflict met in Geneva to begin the messy process of talking over their differences. Every side knew that finding an easily agreeable solution to such a complicated tangle was going to be difficult. Deciding on which groups ought to be represented at the conference and getting those members to agree to meet in the same room, let alone talk to one another, was a major challenge. As CNN International Diplomatic Editor Nic Robertson commented, "The very fact that we're back here again in Geneva, that both sides are here this time . . . is an indication that there is progress."[4] And, as UN special envoy Staffan de Mistura put it, there were few other alternatives available: "As far as I know, the only Plan B available is return to war—and to an even worse war than we've had so far."[5] Despite the high stakes, few people believed the Geneva talks would solve much or that the cease-fire would last very long.

Sadly, by the end of April, that is exactly what happened, as scores of civilians and fighting troops began dying again as heavy fighting and bombing resumed. More than 200 civilians died in the last week of April alone, more than half of them in rebel-held areas of Aleppo, the UN observers reported.[6]

President Obama announced he was ordering 250 military personnel to the area to join the approximately 50 already in Syria.[7] These were to be Special Operations agents who would work with local rebel groups, training and advising but not directly fighting against Syrian Army forces. At the same time, Russia's military presence in Syria increased dramatically. After announcing the withdrawal of some forces in March, Russian president Vladimir Putin

As the conflict dragged on, each day of fighting brought more death and devastation to Syria and its populace.

instead added more helicopters, capable of attacking at low levels and providing cover for ground troops. The shift appeared to show Russia was placing more soldiers in combat situations than before.

In the meantime, peace talks in Geneva went on, though renewed fighting made it harder for representatives from the warring sides to negotiate. As spring gave way to summer, a return to anything like peace and harmony in Syria seemed far away.

PEACE TALKS AND THE CHALLENGES AHEAD

By the summer of 2016, the real question became: What should happen when fighting begins again? Nobody knew for sure, of course. And another question remained: What is the best way forward for all involved? According to Middle East expert Daniel Byman, for the United States and its allies, very few options exist when it comes to Syria, and "all the options are bad ones."[8]

Many analysts agree the first item on the world's agenda would need to be defeating the ISIS threat. In some ways, that has already begun. Increased cooperation between Russia and the United States in 2015 and 2016 affected ISIS's control in Syria. Many ISIS fighters were killed, and so were several high-level leaders. In Iraq since 2014, ISIS lost nearly 40 percent of its former territory, as well as much of its oil revenue.[9] Even though the group remained a potent fighting force and had strong financial backing, some observers believed it could be defeated in Syria and Iraq. The number of ISIS-inspired and sponsored terrorist attacks around the world in 2015 and 2016 alarmed the international community, and this could lead to increased cooperation against ISIS.

Others still believe attacking only from the air, as the United States has done, will not defeat ISIS. But ground attacks would require a massive military effort, costly in both money and lives. Public support for such a war might be limited. The aftermath, even if the military quickly met all its objectives, including ridding Syria of the Assad regime, would be challenging. The region is filled with groups waiting to fill the power vacuum.

Perhaps an even harder question is what to do about Bashar al-Assad. Assad has stated repeatedly that he has no intention of stepping down. At the same time, the

United States and the Syrian opposition have declared the only acceptable outcome is one in which he is removed from power. With Russian support, it has always appeared Assad intends to battle on indefinitely. Yet even Russia has shown signs its patience is wearing thin. This makes some people hope perhaps some US-Russian agreement could eventually force Assad and his powerful allies out of power. In his place, with international monitoring, perhaps a freely elected government might be allowed to form.

US secretary of state John Kerry has not ruled out the possibility of such a joint international intervention in Syria. "If the Assad regime does not live up to its responsibilities and if the Iranians and the Russians do not hold Assad to the promises that they have made," he said, "then the international community obviously is not going to sit there like fools and watch this. There will be an increase

PLAN B: LET BASHAR STAY

Some have suggested perhaps the most logical solution to stop the bloodshed in Syria is for the United States and other nations to back Bashar al-Assad. As diplomat Ryan Crocker has said, "bad as he is, there is something worse," such as ISIS or some other terrorist organization.[10] There are those who believe that with proper monitoring and incentives, Assad could be convinced to enact serious reforms in Syria.

of activity to put greater pressure on them."[11] No one believes such a changeover would be easy. Traditional religious issues and other pressures in the Middle East will always remain powerful. Yet some historians, such as Christian C. Sahner, point to Lebanon, where years of civil war and sectarian turmoil were overcome to form a relatively peaceful and stable nation. Although he admits that circumstances and conditions of the nations' wars are different, at least Sahner is able to see "promising signs" that "could apply to Lebanon and Syria alike."[12]

Though some held out hope for a positive outcome, the fact remained that fighting in Syria had not ended, even during the cease-fire of 2016. The conflict, in one form or another, appeared as though it could go on for years to come. Such long-term struggles

DO IRAN AND SAUDI ARABIA HOLD THE KEY?

If radical militant Islamists were gone, perhaps the key to solving the serious religious divide in Syria could lie with Sunni-led Saudi Arabia and Shia-ruled Iran. The two nations have backed opposite sides in the Syria conflict for years and are influential players in the Islamic world. They have even suggested they might be willing to talk. If they could find a way to put aside their differences, Sunnis and Shia might be willing to live peacefully together in Syria and elsewhere, as they have in years past.

Syrian migrants waited in a refugee camp in Turkey in April 2016.

are nothing new. The Congolese civil war has raged for 21 years, the Afghanistan war for 37 years, and a conflict in Peru for 36 years.[13]

One idea that has been discussed to ease the suffering of Syrian civilians trapped in the nightmare is the creation of safe or "no fly" zones inside the country. Such areas, established and monitored by an international coalition of nations, would give civilians a place to find shelter, food, and medical help away from the fighting. One such safe zone already exists under Kurdish control in northern Syria on the border with Turkey. Although Turkey disputes the Kurds' right to the territory, it remains a peaceful haven for those who can reach it.

The challenges ahead are daunting. Recent history suggests that in Syria, any attempts by outside powers to bring peace and stability are destined to fail. Yet the Syrian people are tough and resilient, and circumstances can change rapidly. The

TURKEY, A KEY PLAYER

From the beginning, Turkey supported opposition forces fighting the Assad regime, including Islamic jihadists. Turkey has sheltered millions of Syrian refugees and Syrian dissidents, but by April 2016 it had begun sending many of them back and shooting at those who attempted to return.

Syrian soldiers entered the ruined town of Qaryatain after clashing with ISIS soldiers in April 2016.

present conflict began as a struggle against fear and oppression, and there is reason to believe the hope and spirit of the Arab Spring can still succeed.

ESSENTIAL FACTS

MAJOR EVENTS

- In 1970, after decades of political and social instability, Minister of Defense Hafez al-Assad takes power in a bloodless coup, supported by Syria's military.
- In 2000, Hafez al-Assad dies suddenly and his son Bashar takes over as president.
- In March 2011, demonstrators in the city of Deraa are attacked by government military and security forces, igniting anti-Assad protests that escalate into civil war.
- In February 2016, the United States, Russia, and other nations agree to a partial cease-fire in Syria.

KEY PLAYERS

- Bashar al-Assad, president of Syria since 2000, is head of a corrupt and dictatorial government and a military police state that controls every aspect of life in his nation. Since 2011, to stay in power, Assad has battled against multiple forces, including rebel factions of his own people, intent on overthrowing him.

- The Islamic State (ISIS), which rose to prominence in Iraq, is a well-funded and brutal fighting force that uses extreme terror and modern propaganda tools to spread and promote its radical Islamic agenda.
- Russia, the United States, Iran, Saudi Arabia, and Turkey are some of the major nations that have taken active roles in the complicated Syrian conflict.

IMPACT ON SOCIETY

The effect of the Syrian conflict on regional and global stability is enormous. It has created a massive humanitarian crisis. Millions of men, women, and children have been killed, injured, and made homeless during the ongoing violence. Refugees have flooded neighboring nations, whose resources have been strained to the breaking point. Nations around the world have endeavored to help, though some are wary that terrorists may come in alongside the truly needy.

QUOTE

"The majority of the Syrian people—and the Syrian opposition we work with—just want to live in peace, with dignity and freedom. And the day after any military action, we would redouble our efforts to achieve a political solution that strengthens those who reject the forces of tyranny and extremism."

—President Barack Obama, remarks to the nation, September 10, 2013

GLOSSARY

CALIPH
A leader of an Islamic community.

COALITION
A collection of groups or people that have joined together for a common purpose.

COUP
An attempt to overthrow leaders.

DISSIDENT
A person who opposes the official policies of a government.

FACTION
A splinter group that breaks from a larger one and forms its own separate unit, sometimes in conflict with the parent group.

GENOCIDE
The deliberate mass murder of a group of people.

JIHAD

The religious duty in Islam to engage in a spiritual struggle for a cause. Jihad is interpreted by extremist militant groups as a literal, violent struggle against nonbelievers.

PROPAGANDA

Information that carries facts or details slanted to favor a single point of view or political bias.

PROXY

A person or agent authorized or enlisted to act in another's place as a substitute.

REGIME

A governing power.

REPRESSIVE

Holding back or keeping down.

SECTARIAN

Having to do with a particular religious group.

SECULAR

Nonreligious.

ZIONIST

Someone who supports the idea of Israel as the rightful homeland of the Jewish people.

ADDITIONAL RESOURCES

SELECTED BIBLIOGRAPHY

Ajami, Fouad. *The Syrian Rebellion*. Washington, DC: Hoover Institute, 2014. Print.

Erlich, Reese. *Inside Syria: The Backstory of Their Civil War and What the World Can Expect*. Amherst, NY: Prometheus, 2014. Print.

McHugo, John. *Syria: A History of the Last Hundred Years*. New York: New Press, 2015. Print.

Sahner, Christian C. *Among the Ruins: Syria Past and Present*. New York: Oxford UP, 2014. Print.

FURTHER READINGS

Gelfand, Dale Evva. *Syria*. Minneapolis, MN: Abdo, 2013. Print.

Marsico, Kate. *ISIS*. Minneapolis, MN: Abdo, 2016. Print.

WEBSITES

To learn more about Special Reports, visit **booklinks.abdopublishing.com**. These links are routinely monitored and updated to provide the most current information available.

FOR MORE INFORMATION

For more information on this subject, contact or visit the following organization:

UNHCR: The UN Refugee Agency
Case Postale 2500
CH-1211 Genève 2 Dépôt
Switzerland
+41 22 739 8111
http://www.unhcr.org
The UNHCR, established in 1950, coordinates international action to protect refugees around the world.

SOURCE NOTES

CHAPTER 1. ARAB SPRING AND THE BOYS OF DERAA

1. "'Day of Rage' Protest Urged in Syria." *NBC News*. NBC News, 23 Feb. 2011. Web. 28 June 2016.

2. Ian Birrell. "Revealed: The Boy Prankster Who Triggered Syria's Bloody Genocide with Slogans Sprayed in His Schoolyard." *Daily Mail*. Daily Mail, 29 Apr. 2013. Web. 28 June 2016.

3. Ibid.

4. Reese Erlich. *Inside Syria*. Amherst, NY: Prometheus, 2014. Print. 16.

5. John McHugo. *Syria*. New York: New Press, 2015. Print. 225–226.

6. Reese Erlich. *Inside Syria*. Amherst, NY: Prometheus, 2014. Print. 86.

7. Ibid. 84.

8. *The Arab Spring*. Ed. Mark L. Haas and David Lesch. Boulder, CO: Westview, 2012. Print. 89–90.

9. George Petras and Jessica Durando. "The Toll of Syria's 5-Year War." *USA Today*. USA Today, 13 Mar. 2016. Web. 28 June 2016.

CHAPTER 2. THE DEEP ROOTS OF TURMOIL

1. David Fromkin, et al. *Cradle & Crucible: History and Faith in the Middle East*. Washington, DC: National Geographic, 2002. Print. 134, 136–37.

2. John McHugo. *Syria*. New York: New Press, 2015. Print. 65.

3. Ibid. 237.

4. Reese Erlich. *Inside Syria*. Amherst, NY: Prometheus, 2014. Print. 55–57.

5. *The War for Palestine: Rewriting the History of 1948*. Ed. Eugene L. Rogan and Avi Shlaim. New York: Cambridge UP, 2001. Print. 177.

6. "Arab World." *World Bank*. World Bank, 2016. Web. 28 June 2016.

7. Mohammad Hassan Khalil. *Between Heaven and Hell: Islam, Salvation, and the Fate of Others*. New York: Oxford UP. Print. 297.

CHAPTER 3. THE ASSADS—THE LIONS IN DAMASCUS

1. Fouad Ajami. *The Syrian Rebellion*. Washington, DC: Hoover Institute, 2014. Print. 41.

2. Reese Erlich. *Inside Syria*. Amherst, NY: Prometheus, 2014. Print. 69–71.

3. Robin Wright. *Dreams and Shadows: The Future of the Middle East*. New York: Penguin, 2008. Print. 224–228, 233–234.

4. Ian Black. "Syrian Human Rights Record Unchanged under Assad, Report Says." *Guardian*. Guardian, 16 July 2010. Web. 20 June 2016.

5. Fouad Ajami. *The Syrian Rebellion*. Washington, DC: Hoover Institute, 2014. Print. 62–65.

6. Anna Borshchevskaya. "Sponsored Corruption and Neglected Reform in Syria." *Middle East Quarterly*. Middle East Forum, Summer 2010. Web. 28 June 2016.

7. "Syria: Speech by Bashar al-Assad, March 30, 2011." *Al-Bab*. Al-Bab, 30 Mar. 2011. Web. 28 June 2016.

8. "Interview with Syrian President Bashar al-Assad." *Wall Street Journal*. Wall Street Journal, Jan. 2011. Web. 28 June 2016.

9. "World Powers Adopt UN Syria Resolution to End Civil War, but Differences on Assad's Future as Leader Remain." *ABC News*. ABC News, 19 Dec. 2015. Web. 28 June 2016.

CHAPTER 4. A CONSTANTLY SHIFTING WAR

1. "Syrian President Bashar al-Assad: Facing Down Rebellion." *BBC News*. BBC News, 21 Oct. 2015. Web. 28 June 2016.

2. "Syrian Civil War—2012." *Global Security Organization*. Global Security Organization, 2016. Web. 28 June 2016.

3. Hana Salama and Hamit Dardagan. "Stolen Futures: The Hidden Toll of Child Casualties in Syria." *Oxford Research Group*. Oxford Research Group, 24 Nov. 2013. Web. 28 June 2016.

4. Fouad Ajami. *The Syrian Rebellion*. Washington, DC: Hoover Institute, 2014. Print. 77.

5. Adeed Dawisha. *The Second Arab Awakening*. New York: Norton, 2013. Print. 184, 187.

6. "Five Years of War in Syria: What Happened and Where We Are Now." *Guardian*. Guardian, 9 Mar. 2016. Web. 28 June 2016.

7. Reese Erlich. *Inside Syria*. Amherst, NY: Prometheus, 2014. Print. 94.

8. "Remarks by the President in Address to the Nation on Syria." *Office of the Press Secretary*. White House, 10 Sept. 2013. Web. 28 June 2016.

9. Robert Spenser. "State Department Announces Its Willingness to Engage with Islamic Front in Syria." *JihadWatch*. JihadWatch, 17 Dec. 2013. Web. 28 June 2016.

10. Catherine E. Shoichet. "Syria's Rebels: 20 Things You Need to Know." *CNN*. CNN, 6 Sept. 2013. Web. 28 June 2016.

11. "Kurd." *Encyclopaedia Britannica*. Encyclopaedia Britannica, 2016. Web. 28 June 2016.

12. Liz Sly. "Did US Weapons Supplied to Syrian Rebels Draw Russia into the Conflict?" *Independent News*. Independent News, 12 Oct. 2015. Web. 28 June 2016.

13. Ibid.

CHAPTER 5. THE RELIGIOUS DIVIDE

1. "Syria." *CIA World Factbook*. CIA World Factbook, 16 June 2016. Web. 28 June 2016.

2. Hussein Abdulwaheed Amin. "The Origins of the Sunni-Shia Split." *USIslam.org*. USIslam.org, 2015. Web. 28 June 2016.

3. Nicole Bibbins Sedaca. "The Religious Component of the Syrian Conflict." *Georgetown Journal of International Affairs*. Georgetown Journal of International Affairs, 21 June 2013. Web. 28 June 2016.

4. Ibid.

5. Reese Erlich. *Inside Syria*. Amherst, NY: Prometheus, 2014. Print. 91.

6. "Syria's Beleaguered Christians." *BBC News*. BBC News, 25 Feb. 2015. Web. 28 June 2016.

8. Ibid.

9. Sam Jones and Owen Bowcott. "Religious Leaders Say ISIS Persecution of Iraqi Christians Has Become Genocide." *Guardian*. Guardian, 9 Aug. 2014. Web. 28 June 2016.

SOURCE NOTES CONTINUED

10. Sarah Eekhoff Zylstra. "John Kerry: ISIS Is Responsible for Genocide against Christians." *Christianity Today*. Christianity Today, 17 Mar. 2016. Web. 28 June 2016.

CHAPTER 6. THE RISE OF ISIS

1. Robert Fisk. "ISIS." *Independent*. Independent, 19 Nov. 2015. Web. 28 June 2016.

2. Christopher Woolf and Nina Porzucki. "Why Are We Having Such a Hard Time Coming Up with a Name for ISIS." *Public Radio International*. PRI, 8 Jan. 2014. Web. 28 June 2016.

3. "Islamic State Leader Abu Bakr al-Baghdadi Encourages Emigration, Worldwide Action." *Intelligence Group*. Jihadist News, 1 July 2014. Web. 28 June 2016.

4. "The New Face of Terror: ISIS' Rise Pushes Iraq to Brink." *Der Spiegel*. Der Spiegel, 25 June 2014. Web. 28 June 2016.

5. "Caliphate Declaration 'Heresy,' Say Islamists Scholars." *Middle East Eye*. Middle East Eye, 4 July 2014. Web. 28 June 2016.

6. "What Did Abu Bakr al-Baghdadi Say?" *Middle East Eye*. Middle East Eye, 5 July 2014. Web. 28 June 2016.

7. Ray Sanchez, et al. "ISIS Goes Global." *CNN*. CNN, 22 Mar. 2016. Web. 28 June 2016.

8. Ibid.

9. Jim Sciutto, et al. "US Airstrikes Hit ISIS Inside Syria for First Time." *CNN*. CNN, 23 Sept. 2014. Web. 28 June 2016.

10. David Hudson. "President Obama: 'We Will Degrade and Ultimately Destroy ISIL.'" *White House*. White House, 10 Sept. 2014. Web. 28 June 2016.

11. Ed Blanche. "Hammering History." *Middle East* Apr. 2014: 26–29. Print.

CHAPTER 7. A HUMANITARIAN CRISIS

1. "A Syrian Refugee Family's Story." *Asylum Access*. Asylum Access, n.d. Web. 28 June 2016.

2. Priyanka Boghani. "A Staggering New Death Toll for Syria's War." *Frontline*. PBS, 11 Feb. 2016. Web. 28 June 2016.

3. "About the Crisis." *UNOCHA*. UNOCHA, n.d. Web. 28 June 2016.

4. Ibid.

5. Ibid.

6. Lewis Sida, et al. "Evaluation of OCHA Response to the Syria Crisis." *ReliefWeb*. ReliefWeb, 1 Mar. 2016. Web. 28 June 2016.

7. Stephanie Ott. "'I Came to Live in Dignity': Syrian Refugees in the US." *Al Jazeera.* Al Jazeera, 25 Nov. 2015. Web. 28 June 2016.

8. "UN Launches Biggest Humanitarian Appeal." *UNOCHA.* UNOCHA, 16 Dec. 2015. Web. 28 June 2016.

9. "Remarks by the President in Address to the Nation on Syria." *Office of the Press Secretary.* White House, 10 Sept. 2013. Web. 28 June 2016.

10. Holly Young. "Guardian Research Suggests Mental Health Crisis among Aid Workers." *Guardian.* Guardian, 23 Nov. 2015. Web. 28 June 2016.

11. "Syria Regional Refugee Response." *UNHCR.* UNHCR, n.d. Web. 28 June 2016.

12. Michael Martinez. "Which Countries Take In the Syrian Refugees?" *CNN.* CNN, 10 Sept. 2015. Web. 28 June 2016.

13. Laura Smith-Spark. "Merkel Calls for Migrant Quotas for EU States to Combat Crisis." *CNN.* CNN, 8 Sept. 2014. Web. 28 June 2016.

14. Rick Gladstone. "Charities Say US Should Take Tens of Thousands of Syrians." *New York Times.* New York Times, 15 Sept. 2015. Web. 28 June 2016.

15. Allison Thompson. "OPED: Saving Lives Amid World's Worst Humanitarian Crisis." *York Dispatch.* York Dispatch, 11 Feb. 2016. Web. 28 June 2016.

16. "Syria War: UN Urges Leaders to Accept More Refugees." *Al Jazeera.* Al Jazeera, 30 Mar. 2016. Web. 28 June 2016.

17. Arnie Seipel. "30 Governors Call For Halt to US Resettlement of Syrian Refugees." *NPR.* NPR, 17 Nov. 2015. Web. 28 June 2016.

18. "Syria: 'Time to End This Horrendous War' Says ICRC President." *ICRC.* ICRC, 26 Feb. 2016. Web. 28 June 2016.

CHAPTER 8. WHAT'S NEXT?

1. Karen DeYoung. "US, Russia and Other Powers Agree on 'Cessation of Hostilities' in Syria." *Washington Post.* Washington Post, 11 Feb. 2011. Web. 28 June 2016.

2. "Remarks by the President on Progress against ISIL." *US State Department.* US State Department, 25 Feb. 2016. Web. 28 June 2016.

3. Ari Soffer. "Syrian FM Threatens 'Surprises' for Western Forces." *Arutz Sheva.* Israeli International News Service, 27 Aug. 2013. Web. 28 June 2016.

4. Holly Yan. "Syrian Peace Talks: Why This Round Might Be Different." *CNN.* CNN, 14 Mar. 2016. Web. 28 June 2016.

5. Ibid.

6. Deutsche Welle. "UN Reports Dire Days in Aleppo as Airstrikes in Syria Destroy Hospital." *Daily News Egypt.* Daily News Egypt, 29 Apr. 2016. Web. 28 June 2016.

7. Michael D. Shear. "US to Increase Military Presence in Syria, Obama Says." *New York Times.* New York Times, 25 Apr. 2016. Web. 28 June 2016.

8. Daniel Byman. "Six Bad Options for Syria." *Washington Quarterly* 38.4 (Winter 2016): 172. Print.

9. Daniel Byman. "ISIS Goes Global—Fight the Islamic State by Targeting Its Affiliates." *Foreign Affairs* 95.2 (March/April 2016): 81. Print.

10. Daniel Byman. "Six Bad Options for Syria." *Washington Quarterly* 38.4 (Winter 2016): 180. Print.

11. "Russia Keeps Bombing Despite Syria Truce; Assad Vows to Fight On." *Reuters.* Reuters, 12 Feb. 2016. Web. 28 June 2016.

12. Christian C. Sahner. *Among the Ruins: Syria Past and Present.* New York: Oxford UP, 2014. Print. 175–177, 179–180.

13. Kenneth Pollack. "Fight or Flight: America's Choice in the Middle East." *Foreign Affairs.* Foreign Affairs, Mar./Apr. 2016. Web. 28 June 2016.

INDEX

ABOUT THE **AUTHOR**

Michael Capek lives in Kentucky with his wife and two children. A former teacher who writes about history and current global issues, the Syrian crisis is of particular interest and concern to him, especially the plight of millions of men, women, and children who are suffering and homeless because of the conflict. Michael sees parallels to the current situation in his own family, because his grandparents were refugees from Europe in the early 1900s.